Imaginary Portraits of the World's Most Famous Felines

Terri Epstein and
Judy Epstein Gage

Illustrated by Roger Roth

A BIRCH LANE PRESS BOOK
PUBLISHED BY CAROL PUBLISHING GROUP

A Birch Lane Press Book
Published by Carol Publishing Group
Birch Lane Press is a registered trademark of Carol Communications, Inc.
Editorial Offices: 600 Madison Avenue, New York, N.Y. 10022
Sales and Distribution Offices: 120 Enterprise Avenue, Secaucus, N.J. 07094
In Canada: Canadian Manda Group, P.O. Box 920, Station U, Toronto, Ontario M8Z 5P9
Queries regarding rights and permissions should be addressed to Carol
Publishing Group, 600 Madison Avenue, New York, N.Y. 10022

Carol Publishing Group books are available at special discounts for bulk
purchases, sales promotions, fund-raising, or educational purposes.
Special editions can be created to specifications. For details, contact Special
Sales Department, Carol Publishing Group, 120 Enterprise Avenue, Secaucus, N.J. 07094

Designed by Paul and Dolores Gamarello

Manufactured in the United States of America
10 9 8 7 6 5 4 3 2 1

Library of Congress Cataloging-in-Publication Data

Epstein, Terri.
     The cat hall of fame : imaginary portraits and profiles of the
world's most famous felines / by Terri Epstein and Judith Epstein
Gage; illustrated by Roger Roth.
          p.   cm.
     "A Birch Lane Press Book."
     ISBN 1-55972-254-1
     1. Cats—Humor.   2. Cats—Caricatures and cartoons.   I. Gage,
Judith Epstein.   II. Roth, Roger.   III. Title.
PN6231.C23E67   1994
818' .5402—dc20   94-12614
                                                              CIP

Contents

Dedication

To Harrison, Hannah, and Jon with more love and appreciation than they can imagine. And to Max, my inspiration.— T.P.E.

To Mollie, Isaiah, and David, with love and gratitude.— J.E.G.

In loving memory of "Auntie Mabe" of West Wardsboro, Vermont, and her famous feline companion "Sammy."— R.R.

Acknowledgments

There are a number of people who have supported us in the writing and production of this book and to whom our thanks are due. Roger Roth, our illustrator, who brought our vision to life; our agent, Jeff Sass at Troma Licensing, who brought us together with Carol Publishing; Steven Schragis and our editor, Kevin McDonough, at Carol Publishing for their enthusiastic and unwavering support; our husbands, Jon Epstein and David Gage, who rose to the occasion without being asked and saw extra time with the children as a perk of parenting and marriage rather than a chore; our children, Harrison, Hannah, Mollie, and Isaiah, who sat by patiently and proudly as the book came together; and our parents, family members, friends, and babysitters who stepped in when needed and encouraged us along the way.

For help on day-to-day details and research of the book, we'd like to extend our thanks to Dan Alterman; Elizabeth Bodner, DVM; Nancy Carozza; Sherry Suib Cohen; Robin Davis; Lee Ducat; Andy Gurney; Terry Hildebrandt; Gloria Jacobs; Susan Kempler; Paul Korshin; Liwah Lai; David Lenkowsky; Barbara Marcus; Chris McManimon; Lisa McNees; Viola Penrose; Sprocket Royer; Marcia Schlaaf; Julie Senack; Debra Thomas; Hildy Tow; Mike Weatherly; and Jan Winarsky.

Preface

Watch a cat long enough and you'll undoubtedly notice human characteristics mirrored in its feline mannerisms. Cats' distinctive personalities and physical attributes lend themselves to both whimsical imagery and improbable musings about possible "other lives." It is the fantasy of these "other lives" that we have set out to capture in *The Cat Hall of Fame*.

This collection of pun-inspired characters grew out of our fantasies about Max and Critter, the cats in our lives, imagining who they might have been, or might yet become within the course of their nine lives. In some cases, we came upon the pun, then created the illusion. In others, we came upon the image, obscured by a human façade, then developed the play on words.

There was Critter in a seductive stretch awakening from her catnap, and she suddenly resembled Lady Catterly outstretched across her lover's lap. Then there was Max, whose studied gaze transformed him into Mewzart, contemplating his next orchestral composition. A neighbor's lovely yet feisty feline conjured the image of Katharine Hepurrn. The pedigreed lap cat down the hall evoked Marie Catoinette, feasting on paw-size petit fours.

Conversely, there have been moments when some unsuspecting human became transformed into a fanciful, feline image. When Winston Churchill became Winston Purrchill, a posturing, pensive British shorthair. When Liza Minelli became Liza Mewnelli, meowing at the moon. Or when Joe DiMaggio sending one over the wall became Joe DiMewggio batting at a ball of yarn.

Once inspired, the images came quickly, cropping up at every other odd and ordinary turn. Saks immediately became Cats Fifth Avenue. Late night became time for David Litterman. Morning wasn't morning without Willard Scatt and his weather. And no Sunday passed without the *Mew York Times*.

But what to do with it all? *The Cat Hall of Fame* and the legend of *The Theory of Reincat-nation*, is our way of sharing the fun and fantasy inherent in the myth of a cat's nine lives.

Established by us, the creators, with the welcomed addition of illustrator Roger Roth, our *Cat Hall of Fame*—complete with imaginary edifice and founding fable—now exists proud in its resolve to induct a variety of *purrsonalities*, representing all walks of any and all lives from the popular to the fairly obscure, all in an effort to satisfy cat lovers, like ourselves, of a broad and varied range of interests.

We hope you enjoy your visit.

FALL 1994

Introduction

This cat tale begins in 1912, when a small, frightened child from Kiev arrived in America newly orphaned, clinging to the only thing left of her former life, her beloved cat, Natasha. A survivor of the *Titanic* disaster, the little girl who would later become a wealthy New York socialite and Founder of The Cat Hall of Fame, was emigrating with her family to the United States when the celebrated ship went down.

Mrs. Edward Randolph, the wife of a prominent New York banker, was also making the famed maiden voyage returning from a holiday on the Continent. Charmed by young Sophia shortly after embarking, Mrs. Randolph became acquainted with her family, learned of the czarist pogroms that had caused them to flee Russia and offered to help with their resettlement arrangements when they arrived in New York.

While the ship was being evacuated after the notorious iceberg was struck, Mrs. Randolph watched in horror as the lifeboat carrying Sophia, her mother, and her sister was toppled by others struggling to climb to safety. She reached out frantically from her own lifeboat to save them but was only able to grab Sophia, clutching the family cat, before seeing the others perish in the icy waters. Hugging the crying, shivering child, she wept as she witnessed the crippled ship, with Sophia's father and brother still on board, disappear beneath the dark, silent sea. Looking toward the star-filled heavens, Mrs. Randolph vowed to protect Sophia, to love her as her own child and to give her the life her parents had so desperately wanted in America.

Upon arriving in New York amidst much chaos surrounding the disastrous event, Sophia and her cat were immediately taken to the Randolph home—a stately mansion on Fifth Avenue—where Edward Randolph fell instantly in love with the sad-eyed child. She was welcomed into their lives, and in due time was legally adopted becoming the adored only child of the wealthy couple, nurtured, loved and cherished throughout a very privileged life.

Raised in the upper strata of Manhattan society, Sophia Randolph attended the finest schools including Miss Grace's Academy for Young Girls, the Spence School and Vassar

College. Marked by unusual beauty and a deeply-felt—though quietly manifested—*joie de vivre*, she was popular with her peers and very much pursued by young men from neighboring schools. A bright and dedicated student, however, she preferred her studies and the company of her cats (Natasha and her nine offspring!) to the frivolous social activities of a coed's life. It was no surprise then when Natasha died—during Sophia's senior year in college—that she would plunge into a deep depression, mourning the loss of the nineteen-year-old cat, her constant companion since childhood and the only connection to her birth family lost at sea.

Refusing all company for the remainder of the year, Sophia retreated into her studies becoming more and more dependent on her cats for comfort and companionship. By graduation she had become thoroughly convinced that the world would be far greater if inhabited fully by felines with their quiet, intelligent, unintrusive manner. With this notion as the nucleus of her studies, she embarked on an advanced degree at Harvard in the Animal Behavior program pursuing her fascination with all things feline and the conceptualization of her feline point of view.

After three years of earnest study, Sophia's fantasy of a feline world finally found its way into theoretical form and was presented in her master's thesis as *The Theory of Reincatnation: The Manifestations of the Feline Nine-Life Cycle Within the Context of the Human Landscape*.

The theory suggested that the feline species, with its characteristic poise, independence, expressiveness, intelligence, and tenaciousness, represented the highest form of civilization and moral development—the species by which all others should be measured. She grounded her theory in the discovery that all great men and women throughout the history of the world—including world leaders, artists, entertainers, scientists, etc.—exhibited pronounced feline traits and qualities, suggesting that they had been transfigured during the course of the nine-life cycle from the feline to the human form. In other words, dismantle the human façade and the cat within will make itself evident.

Up until this point in her theoretical explication, Sophia had been greeted by her academic colleagues with bemusement and critical tolerance. It was her closing remarks, however—the suggestion that the world would be far better off if *reincatnated* on a mass basis—that caused her colleagues to dismiss her as academically absurd and to charge that her theory was utter fantasy.

It was at this juncture that Sophia met the dashing Philip DeNeuf, a graduate student who shared her affinity for the fantastic and heard her theory as both daring and progressive in a field dominated by the traditional and unimaginative. He courted her passionately, asking her to marry him after only three months, so taken was he by her spirited intelligence and beauty. Although it was a well-known quirk of their relationship that he was a devotee of dogs and she a fancier of felines, Sophia became enchanted by Philip's utter devotion. She accepted his proposal and the two were married in New York, where they settled, taking over the west wing of the Randolph residence.

Despite her strong academic tendencies, the newly-married Mrs. DeNeuf put aside her feline studies, deferring instead to her husband's canine interests as he rose in his field at a variety of prestigious New York institutions before founding the now internationally-recognized American Canine Association. During the "dog" years, Mrs. DeNeuf contented herself with the matters of motherhood, deriving joy and satisfaction from her daughters, Anna and Alexandra, (named for her mother and sister, lost at sea) with whom she shared close and loving relationships.

It wasn't until Philip died of a stroke in 1989 that Sophia DeNeuf showed signs of returning to her feline studies. Within weeks of the funeral, she had cleared out both closets and canines selling off the DeNeuf Kennels along with the prized pair of pinschers that had guarded their home. Concentrating on the aged, ill, and infirmed—those difficult to place in adoptive homes—she then began taking in homeless cats from shelters in large numbers, adding to the five generations of Natasha's offspring that had remained her only feline ties throughout the years of her marriage. With plenty of room to spare, Sophia DeNeuf found it increasingly difficult to turn away any cat in need.

It was when the tally of tails reached eighty-two that Anna DeNeuf, the eldest of the DeNeuf daughters, began putting the pieces together. "Although she tried to hide it, Mother had always continued reading in her field—reading, taking notes, clipping articles and filing everything away in her private study, the smaller library she maintained adjacent to her bedroom. She did a lot of writing there as well, more so as we grew older

13

and whenever Father was away on business. We always assumed it had to do with her academic work."

"Publically Mother had abandoned her feline studies," continued Alexandra, "so as not to jeopardize Father's standing in the canine community. But we often found feline-related journals and books tucked away in her rooms. When Father died and she began bringing homeless cats into the mansion—in addition to Natasha's 18 descendants!—We began to suspect that she was getting close to openly resuming her academic work now that it would have no consequences where Father was concerned."

The girls' suspicions were soon confirmed. During the spring of 1990, about three months after their father's death, Sophia DeNeuf called her daughters into her study and told them of her lifelong dream, a dream she'd nourished privately throughout her years of marriage. Her dream, as she described it, was to found an institution devoted to the spirit of her *Theory of Reincatnation*, an institution that would celebrate cats and the manifestations of their remarkable nine-life cycles, an institution to be called The Cat Hall of Fame.

"It was incredible!" remembered Anna DeNeuf. "All those years hosting Canine Association cocktail receptions, always so gracious and accommodating, when her heart was still so irrevocably connected to cats!"

After describing her vision of the Hall as a place that would pay tribute to the feline species *and* serve as an educational center, Sophia DeNeuf asked the girls if they would object to the mansion being used as the site. Assuring them that ample space would remain as private living quarters, she went on to ask if they would join in her unusual pursuit and serve as directors of the project. Flattered and proud to be included in their mother's dream, they agreed without hesitation to be part of it.

The three women spent the next month formalizing the plans that would result in the realization of the elder DeNeuf's lifelong dream. A good deal of the groundwork had already been completed. According to O. R. Davenport, a longtime friend and confidante, as well as Mrs. DeNeuf's personal attorney, The Cat Hall of Fame was a project she'd been devoted to for years. Having been involved in a confidential and advisory capacity since its inception Davenport recalled "many years of quiet effort put forth in the planning of the Hall."

Once Mrs. DeNeuf had let the proverbial cat out of the bag—to her daughters, that is—the Hall quickly began to take shape. In little less than three months, with the DeNeuf daughters overseeing the administrative concerns, architects had been brought in to begin planning the renovation that would render the mansion suitable for public use. In addition, a team of lawyers and financial advisors had been created, led by Mr. Davenport, to oversee investments pertaining to The Cat Hall of Fame and the Foundation that would be created to maintain the Hall and fund its educational programs.

Meanwhile, Sophia DeNeuf set out on an expedition to expand her own personal collection of cat-related antiques, artifacts and memorabilia that would serve as the basis for The Cat Hall of Fame Collection. Unaccustomed to traveling alone, she asked her best friend from childhood, Mrs. Mamie Rothschild, to join her. Mrs. Rothschild's own husband had died only seven months prior to Philip DeNeuf's death and she welcomed the unconventional diversion.

Upon their return, and with the collection of artifacts and memorabilia well underway, Mrs. DeNeuf and her daughters began the search for an official portraitist for the Hall, an artist who would produce formal portraits of the extraordinary felines inducted into The Cat Hall of Fame. The portraits would be displayed in the Grande Rotunda—the mansion's enormous and elaborate central foyer connecting the four wings of the DeNeuf home—serving as the centerpiece of The Cat Hall of Fame Collection.

A noted patron of the arts, having served on several boards including that of the Metropolitan Art Museum and the New York Ballet Company, Mrs. DeNeuf was well-prepared for the task. She was known for her staunch support of upcoming, inspired members of the arts community and with the plans for The Cat Hall of Fame always in mind, she had kept track of any artist she thought suitable for the portraitist position once the time came to fill it.

Working from her files, she chose eleven candidates, meeting with each individually to discuss the Hall and to explain what the job would entail. She placed great emphasis on the dedication and commitment the position would require explaining that continuity—a consistency of style in the portraits—was of great importance. Not interested in presenting a hodgepodge of portraits, sketches, and photographs found in other collections, she made it clear that the artist chosen would be expected to remain an ongoing and integral part of The Cat Hall of Fame, in essence, a member of the family.

Eight of the eleven artists interviewed were interested and went on to prepare sample portraits while Mrs. DeNeuf, along with Mrs. Rothschild, set out on a second acquisitions trip to Europe. The samples were to be submitted upon her return with a final decision to follow a week later. It was then that the tragedy occurred.

On April 8, 1993, Anna DeNeuf received a call from a distraught Mrs. Rothschild with the news that Sophia had been killed in a freak scaffolding collapse at the Palace of Versailles. Devastated by their mother's tragic death, Anna and Alexandra DeNeuf put the Hall on hold until, at the prodding of Mrs. Rothschild and Mr. Davenport, it became clear that only the continuation of their work—and the fulfillment of their mother's dream— would fill the void left by her death. And so, with the renovation of the DeNeuf mansion nearly complete and the knowledge that their mother would be deeply disappointed if the Hall didn't open as scheduled, they moved swiftly and with great determination to bring the project back on schedule for the fall 1994 Gala Opening Celebration and Initial Induction Ceremony their mother had anticipated.

The first matter of business was to publicly announce the establishment of The Cat Hall of Fame. Organizing a press reception in the Grande Rotunda of the DeNeuf mansion, the DeNeuf daughters unveiled the plans for New York's first institution devoted solely to felines and presented the architectural blueprints for the renovation of the mansion that would serve as its site. Recounting their mother's academic achievements, they gave a thorough explanation of her *Theory of Reincatnation*, the idea upon which the Hall was founded.

Mrs. DeNeuf's personal background, especially her survival of the sinking of the Titanic and the loss of her family (with the exception of Natasha, her cat), was the highpoint of interest until Mr. Davenport was introduced to make the bequest announcement. Introduced as a partner of Davenport & Hughes, a trusted friend and legal advisor, and the executor of their mother's will, he revealed Mrs. DeNeuf's extraordinary bequest of $52 million, funds earmarked for the specific purpose of ensuring the future development of Sophia DeNeuf's feline legacy, The Cat Hall of Fame.

"The funds," Davenport announced, "are to be used for the completion of the renovation project already underway, continued acquisitions, the establishment of an on-site educational center and all staffing needs."

As expected, the press went wild. In papers everywhere the next morning the headlines read, "Millionairess Leaves Millions to Honor Cats." It was a twist on the age-old story of the old woman leaving millions *to* her cats, and the press pounced on it to the delight of the DeNeuf daughters.

Five months passed and enormous strides were taken in the formalization of the facilities, staffing, and proposed events, and exhibitions. On October 20, 1993, the DeNeuf daughters, now officially Cochairpersons of The Cat Hall of Fame, arranged another press reception at the mansion to announce several key staff appointments including the curator, the director of development and an official inductee portraitist.

Chosen as the Hall's curator was Natalie Claudeau, a graduate of Smith College and The New York Institute of Fine Arts where she wrote her doctoral dissertation on "Fantasy and Romanticism in the Feline Images of Henri Rousseau." Ms. Claudeau, who began her curating career at the Mount Holyoke College Museum of Art, had distinguished herself as an expert in late nineteenth and twentieth century art. After eight years she had left the academic environment to become head of the Department of Painting and Drawing at the New York Museum of Contemporary Art where she was credited with enlarging the museum's collection of both Rousseau and Picasso, making it competitive with similar institutions around the world.

At the press conference where the announcements were made, Anna DeNeuf, a former college roommate of the Hall's new curator, expressed her delight at having won Ms. Claudeau's services, pointing out that the Metropolitan Art Museum had also been courting her for their Early Twentieth Century Art department. When asked to comment on her new position, Ms. Claudeau responded with marked enthusiasm saying, "I'm terribly excited by the prospect of opening an entirely new and heretofore unknown collection of feline-related art and returning to the work I was so drawn to earlier in my career."

Appointed as Director of Development was Maxwell Chatham, former Director of the

Rittenhouse Collection, the small yet prestigious institution in Philadelphia, similarly created through a bequest of one of the city's social patrons.

Mr. Chatham had been a fixture in the city's arts circles having spent his entire professional life within its institutions. A graduate of the University of Pennsylvania with a degree in Archaeology, he began his career as a researcher at the University Museum heading up a project tracing the feline presence in civilizations from the pre-Egyptian to the Classic Greek periods. Frustrated when a cutback in funding brought a premature end to his study, Chatham returned to the classroom earning an MBA from the Wharton School, and embarked on a career in development as an assistant director at the Rodin Foundation.

He later joined the Philadelphia Institute of Fine arts where he rose to Director of Development and instituted a "Silent Patrons" program designed to rally much needed corporate support. The success of his program resulted in an invitation from the more intimate Rittenhouse Collection to head up its foundation, where he established a similar program to assure its growth.

Asked why he had decided to leave Philadelphia after so many years, Chatham replied, "It's time to move on to new challenges, new circles, new subjects, to a new life really. The Cat Hall of Fame offers all of that. And New York offers everything else!"

Roger Roth, an illustrator schooled at Pratt Institute in Brooklyn, New York, was named the Official Cat Hall of Fame Portraitist. He won the position after submitting a full portfolio of feline figures, followed by two sample portraits prepared to the specifications laid out during his meeting with Mrs. DeNeuf just before her untimely death.

"We chose Mr. Roth for a number of reasons," explained Alexandra DeNeuf at the press conference, "not the least of which was his wonderful, subtle sense of humor—very much like our mother's."

Added Anna DeNeuf, "We were also taken by his soft use of the pencil in concert with his watercolors, and by his seemingly innate ability to capture the personalities of his feline subjects."

Roth had worked as a freelance illustrator for a variety of publications including the *New York Times*, the *Wall Street Journal*, *Family Circle* and *Sports Illustrated*. He had also illustrated several books, one of which he also authored, and had been widely recognized for his work. When asked by a reporter what his initial response was upon hearing the good news, Roth replied with a chuckle, "Call my agent."

Finally in early September 1994, with the renovation project completed and the initial collection of portraits a *fait accompli*, Anna and Alexandra DeNeuf, along with their chosen board of trustees including Mr. Davenport and Mrs. Rothschild, issued formal invitations to over five hundred individuals, corporations, arts and educational institutions, and members of the press to attend the Gala Opening and Initial Induction Ceremony of The Cat Hall of Fame.

Held on October 21, 1994, the event was an elegant affair with cocktails, champagne, and hors d'oeuvres served on the veranda of the inner courtyard at 6 P.M., the induction ceremony at 7 P.M. in the Grande Rotunda where the Offical Inductee Portraits were unveiled, followed by a black-tie dinner dance to the music of the Peter Blakley Orchestra in the Randolph Ballroom until midnight.

With the Gala Opening a success, the DeNeuf daughters realized that they had built a strong foundation for their mother's dream and hoped she would someday enjoy the benefit of her own theory, returning to the Hall, perhaps as an inductee herself, or as a simple watchcat presiding lovingly over her legacy, prowling the halls of her own creation.

The Hall

Located in the heart of New York City, the Cat Hall of Fame is a spectacular salute to famous and infamous felines from every nation and historic period.

Housed in the former residence of its founder, the late Sophia Randolph DeNeuf, the animal behaviorist noted for the *Theory of Reincatnation*, the Hall consists of several permanent galleries and exhibition spaces that serve as showcases for its collection of inductee portraits and memorabilia.

Among the Hall's highlights are the Pawlitzer Library and Reference Room with its growing collection of feline-related rare books and manuscripts. Included is the original draft of Ernest Hemingcat's Pawlitzer Prize–winning *The Old Cat and the Sea*, the letters of Lady Catterly's lover, and the correspondence between Sigmund Fureud and Albert Felinestein.

The Cat Hall of Fame Theater, located on the Hall's lower level, is devoted to the accomplishments of film industry inductees and offers special film programs in the evenings and on weekends. For the Hall's opening, there will be a continous showing of *Catsablanca*, *Catbaret*, *Mary Pawppins*, and a retrospective of films starring Katharine Hepurrn.

The Hall's main attraction, however, is the Grande Rotunda, a cavernous and elaborately decorated space that serves as the formal gallery of inductee portraits. Inductees represent an array of purrsonalities and are selected by the board of trustees upon the recommendations of a five-member research committee. Each of the formal portraits on display, commissioned to immortalize the inductees selected, will remain a part of the Hall's permanent collection. This catalog, published as a commemorative edition, marks the Hall's gala opening and includes the complete collection of portraits on display.

The Cat Hall of Fame also offers refreshments at either of two dining spots. The *Finicky Café* is a full-service restaurant situated just off the Grande Rotunda. *Take Paws*, which offers lighter fare, is located on the lower level and opens onto the Hall's Path of Pawprints Sculpture Garden for outdoor dining when weather permits.

The Cat Hall of Fame is open Tuesday through Sunday from 10 A.M. to 6 P.M. and until noon on Fridays. For information about educational programs, contact the Hall's administrative offices.

The Cat Hall of Fame statuette, a marble reproduction of the original landmark statue, is presented, along with a Certificate of Induction, to each inductee at the annual Cat Hall of Fame Induction Ceremony. The original statue can be seen at the Cat Hall of Fame in New York, in the Path of Pawprints Sculpture Garden along with the statue of Napawleon Bonaparte and other notable feline works of art.

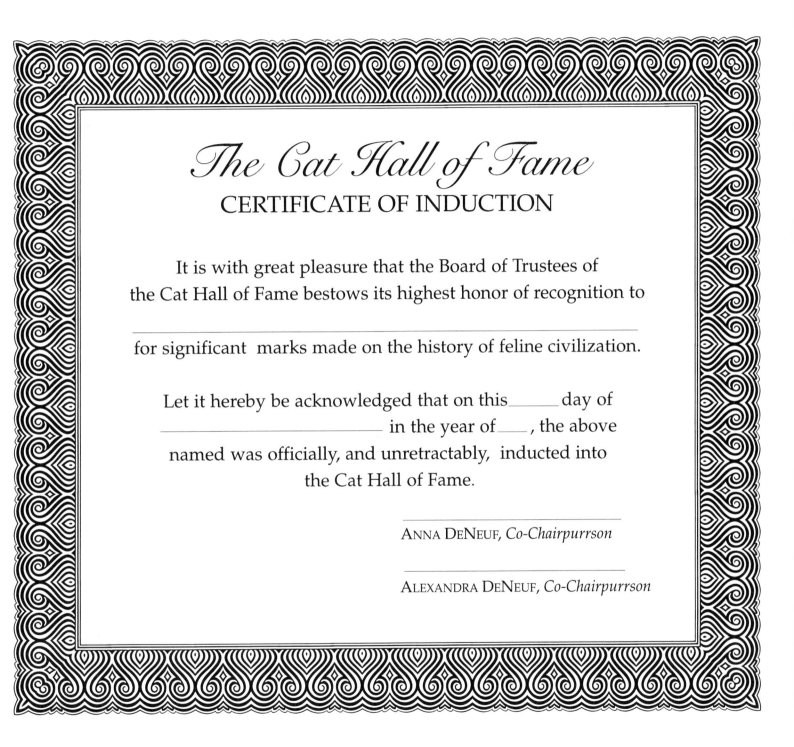

The Cat Hall of Fame
CERTIFICATE OF INDUCTION

It is with great pleasure that the Board of Trustees of
the Cat Hall of Fame bestows its highest honor of recognition to

_____

for significant marks made on the history of feline civilization.

Let it hereby be acknowledged that on this_____ day of
_____ in the year of ___ , the above
named was officially, and unretractably, inducted into
the Cat Hall of Fame.

_____
ANNA DENEUF, *Co-Chairpurrson*

_____
ALEXANDRA DENEUF, *Co-Chairpurrson*

The Portrait Collection

Mewhammad Alley
1942 –

The most revered, recognizable, and controversial sports feline of his generation, Mewhammad Alley found himself castigated by critics in one life while fulfilling the fantasies of fans in another. A boxer who's forced up a hairball or two from many an opponent, Alley is fabled for his extraordinary eye-paw coordination, his dazzling dance, and powerful pounce.

Alley's reign, which began with the gold at the 1960 Olympics, lasted through his final title bout in 1978 when he recaptured the heavyweight crown for a record-breaking third time. Along the way, he outboxed many a challenger including the feisty felines Sonny Hisston, Joe Furazier, and George Furman, with lots of fur flying but barely a mark made on Alley's nearly perfect puss.

Celebrated as well for his self-proclaimed invincibility, Alley often expressed himself in—of all things!—*doggerel* verse, and made his boast, "I am the Greatest!" his purrsonal and professional cry.

As his record plainly shows, he *is* one champion whose actions spoke as loudly as his purrs. Fighting first as Catsius Mewcellus Clay, Alley's deeply felt and displayed faith led to the formal adoption of his Muslim name, and to his refusal to be drafted into the Vietnam War. Convicted in 1967 of violating the Selective Service Act, he found himself barred from the ring, flayed of his title, and persecuted by a previously purring press, with the exception of his longtime supporter, Howard Catsell.

From 1971 on, however, with his conviction overturned and his reinstatement into boxing official, Alley recaptured both his public and his pride after title bout knockouts of champs George Furman and Leon Sphinx. With three Heavyweight Championships under his belt, Alley retired to a Michigan farm where he remains, to this day, the sacred idol of his devoted fans.

Napawleon Bonaparte

1769 – 1821

With guillotine blades falling at the least provocation, and catfights erupting in alleys and fields, France in the late eighteenth century was a domestic mess. The common breeds had stormed the Bastille and the long-reigning monarchy had been overthrown (with heads of state in a basket as proof!). Life was anything but claw and order.

Enter Napawleon Bonaparte, the little mixed-breed with big ideas. A tiger in his own mind, though he stood only one-foot-three (on two paws!), Napawleon—from the start—exhibited ambition even his own allies feared. With grand political aspirations, (which would eventually lead to his coronation as Empurror of France, *twice*!) he pounced on Europe, sinking tenacious claws into any territory he coveted, i.e. all of it.

A brilliant strategist, Napawleon won the support of the countrycats by devising a government that at once pacified *their* revolutionary demands while obscuring the broad authority it granted *him*. Legions of felines who willingly conscripted, fueled the many successes of their Empurrer's furocious expansion of the Empire.

With victories the norm, including his most stunning triumph at Austerlitz in 1805, Napawleon faced defeat with a snarl. During his disastrous Russian campaign he led his forces to the very outskirts of Mousecow only to have their paws freeze in the snow. When defeat at Leipzig followed the catastrophic retreat from Russia in 1812, he returned to Paris with a pout on his puss and was forced to abdicate the "throne" he himself had created and accept banishment to the Isle of Elba.

Although he'd rally once more after two years in exile, Napawleon's reinstatement would last only One Hundred Days. France, infested with malcontents by that time, refused Napawleon the corps of cats needed to stave off enemy breeds at the borders. Decisively defeated at Waterloo, at the paws of Britain's Wellington in 1815, Napawleon was finally overthrown, removed from power, and sent packing to St. Helena, a broken cat.

Although his impurrial escapades would end in disgrace, and his life would end in exile, interest in the Empurrer's exploits re-emerged, creating a legend that's grown larger than life, certainly larger than the cat himself!

To this day, any tiny but ambitious Tom cat or over-reaching, diminutive stray is said to have a "Napawleon Complex." In fact, the very image of Napawleon, claws tucked tightly inside his uniform has become synonymous with someone afflicted with delusions of grandeur, a crazy cat whose reach far exceeds his paws.

NAPAWLEON

Marie Catoinette
1755 – 1793

*I*t was during troubled times in Paris that Marie Catoinette became Queen of France. Frivolous, kittenish, and an enemy of reform, she disturbed the rest of the common breeds, provoking the revolutionary movement of 1789 and the fall of the French monarchy three years later.

Her King, Mewis XVI, proved to be the pussy of the pair, while Catoinette, the Austrian tigress, sought fun and games with her circle of foolish, foppish felines. Her purchasing of costly court toys combined with continued retractions of the court's clawing attempts at reform, marked the monarchy for ruin and caused the Queen's enemies to spread scandalous reports of her alleged tomcatting. The most infamous of these episodes, the Diamond Collar Affair, found her in an unnatural relationship with a red-crested Cardinal, which further discredited the monarchy.

Unable to grasp that France's legions of litters needed kibble, not cake, the Queen ignored the pawcity of food stock, resisted the abolition of feudalism, and continued to exercise an untethered Royal purrogative. This left her prey to popular agitators who, after the historic stalking of the Bastille—a symbol of royal despawtism—captured her and her incompetent king while returning to Paris from their palace at Fursailles.

Subsequently attempting to flee, disguised as Russian shorthairs, the royal pair was seized and brought back to Paris where Catoinette, and her now fraidy-cat King, made one last effort to reposition the crown. Alas, with peasants' and Parliament's backs up, insurrection was at paw and the monarchy was overthrown. The King lost his last life at the guillotine immediately; Catoinette's head rolled shortly thereafter.

Catsablanca

1942

102 minutes/black & white

A classic 1940s film starring Humfurry Bogart and Ingrid Purrgman, this story of wartime romance and espionage has been ranked as one of Hollywood's best-loved pictures.

Winner of three Acatemy Awards, including Best Picture and Best Director, the story is set in war-torn Catsablanca, a city teeming with European refugees during World War II. Humfurry Bogart, playing Rick, the suave, cigarette-smoking, American night-club owner, plays host to all, with allegiances to none, remaining aloof at all times.

The plot thickens when Purrgman, a lover from a past life, arrives at Rick's with her Resistance-hero husband (Paw Henreid) on the prowl for visas to Lisbon. Romantic embers are stirred and passion purrs again, with scene after scene of now classic, cinematic gazes.

This legendary film, loved by legions of feline fans for its multitude of memorable moments—not the least of which is the foggy farewell scene pictured here—has also left a legacy of lines that will be meowed for years, among them, "We'll always have Purris" and "Here's lookin' at you, Kit."

CATS FIFTH AVENUE

Cats Fifth Avenue
1924 –

The finest in feline fashions since 1924, Cats Fifth Avenue has groomed generations of the world's most cosmopolitan cats.

The first of the major Manhattan retailers to move "uptown," the shop opened its magnificent doors in the residential neighborhood of Rockefurllers and Vandercats. In doing so, it established itself as the premier feline outfitter specializing in made-to-order custom designs—shoes, hats, purrses, purrls, catstume jewelry, even uniforms for domestic cats (a velvet cape for kitty's nanny, an upholstery-matching uniform for the chauffur). And, of course, furstyling by the famous French coiffur, Antoine de Purris!

Established for the feminine feline, Cats Fifth Avenue now serves gentlecats and kitties as well—always with the high-quality, fine, and tasteful styles that have become the Cats Fifth Avenue tradition.

The flagship Fifth Avenue store, with its signature awnings, monumental and architecturally significant entrances, and decorative bronze grillwork, remains the centerpiece of this fashion empire and was proudly designated a New York City Historic Landmark in 1986.

General
George S. Catton
1885–1945

Esteemed, albeit controversial, four-star general of the United States Army during World War II, Catton was known for his hard-headed toughness and the fiery temper that nearly got him catmarshalled for slapping a subordinate with his paw. Having clawed his way to the top, he demanded the same diligence and determination from his troops. Through a mixture of fear and admiration, they served as he wished, paying him the respect and loyalty he needed to lead the series of successful campaigns for which he is remembered.

One such campaign was the invasion of North Africa in 1941–42. No pussyfooter, he reveled in rolling out his armored tank divisions scoring early, able victories for the Allies. He later commanded the Sicilian campaign, followed by his legendary sweep across France and Germany in 1944–45, including the Battle of the Bulge.

After surviving countless life-threatening battles, "Old Blood and Catgut" lost the last of his nine lives in a civilian automobile accident in Germany, just months after the war ended. His memoirs, *The War as I Mew It*, and the 1970 Acatemy Award-winning film *Catton* starring George C. Scatt and written by Francis Furd Coppawla, remain testaments to his military achievements and legendary lives.

Betty Crockat

Circa 1950

*T*he quintessential domestic feline of the 1950s, this warm, cuddly calico took pride in tending hearth and home. With heaping teaspoons of TLC and the soft, gentle touch of her paw, she cared for her kitties, feeding and grooming, nursing when sick, teaching good etiquette and posture, and, above all, cultivating their natural instincts.

In addition to her maternal duties were her household chores. These included dusting, vacuuming, laundering, marketing, and mousing, all of which she pounced on with verve and efficiency.

What she enjoyed most, however, was cooking and baking. Betty Crockat *loved* her kitchen! Outfitted with all of the latest appliances, she spent hours baking birthday and bundt cakes, cookies and kuchen, her trusty red spoon always close at paw.

Truly "the housecat of tomorrow," Betty delighted in the convenient new cake mixes of her day, which, she purred contentedly, "allowed her more time for the myriad other household chores that were a housecat's responsibility."

Joe DiMewggio
1914 –

Prowling the park in Clippurr stripes for well over a decade, Joe DiMewggio, the all-Americat wartime sports hero, was one of the greatest all-around players in baseball history.

DiMewggio, one of three sons sired destined to play the majors (a remarkable feat of breeding, itself worthy of Cat Hall of Fame recognition!), was known around the neighborhood as the "Kit with the Mitt." Lured to New York by an offer to play in the Americat League, DiMewggio left the pussycat paradise of Fisherman's Wharf and headed for his new patch of grass in the Bronx. Stalking his urban terrain, this rangy centerfielder covered his territory with the grace and speed of a cheetah. His fluid swing and swift reflexes made any pitch his prey at the plate. No one played the game like broad-pawed Joe!

Affectionately nicknamed Jumpin' Joe, DiMewggio achieved some striking stats: three-time Americat League MVC, .325 lifetime at-bat mark, nine World Series Collars, and an outstanding fifty-six-game hitting streak in '41. Named to the *Baseball* Hall of Fame in 1955, only his short-lived marriage to a famous Hollywood sex-kitten drew more admiration from his heated fans.

A legend in his own time, DiMewggio remains close to the hearts of his many fans and evokes memories of an era long gone—languid spring afternoons lounging near the radio, chewing pawfuls of popcorn, kittens running wild in the yard, and the sportscasters purring:

It's the bottom of the ninth, two on, two out, Clippurrs down by one. Jumpin' Joe pads up to the plate. The Tigers' nifty southpaw pitcher steps onto the mound, looks in for the sign, while DiMewggio stretches his lengthy limbs. The windup, the pitch—it's high and inside, brushing Joe's whiskers and knocking him back on his tail. The crowd is hissing angrily, folks! And Catsey Stengel's pacing in the dugout. Joe slowly licks himself off and digs his paws into the soil. He's set for the next one. The windup, the pitch, CRACK! It's a feeeeeee-line drive, out of the park—and the Clippurrs snag the game. DiMewggio does it again!

41

Cats Domino

1 9 2 8 –

"And now, the one and only, paw-poppin', tail-tappin', whisker-snappin' Cats Domino!"

Since leaping to fame down in Mew Orleans, adoring fans have teemed from the tenements, pranced from the parks, and swung from the suburbs to see this fabulous, fastidious, fat cat—the King of Rhythm and Mews!

One of a litter of nine, Cats walked the ivories as a kitten and quickly learned to play for his supper in the catclubs of Tin Pan Alley. In no time at all, he was off to the recording studio, marking the charts with feline favorites like *The Fat Cat*, *Ain't That a Maim*, *I'm Stalking*, and *Bluepurry Hill*. With sixty-five million records sold and twenty-two Gold Discs on his collar, his purr was recognized around the globe, with only Elvis Purresley out-meowing him! This rockin'-rollin' rascal had become the first black cat to capture the white record world!

Dressed to kill at every purrformance, Cats also became known for his nose for fashion. With an abundance of clams in his coffurs, he could readily indulge his love of stickpins and diamond collars, while collecting the hundreds of socks he required to match his fifty suits! Before stepping on stage, he'd splash himself with exotic scents, then comb and pat his fur into his famous, fluffy twin peak. He *was* the cat's meow!

With a career that stretched across stage and studio, and an instinct for flashy fashions, Cats Domino sired an unpurrecedented style of rhythms *and* rags—a style that remains as indomitable as ever.

42

Isadora Duncat

1878–1927

*I*nnovative American dancer who redefined the conventions of movement, Isadora Duncat challenged traditional schools of dance with her free and natural improvisational style.

Although recognized today as a founding feline of modern dance, Duncat was considered highly controversial at the outset of her career, her performances eliciting hisses from unenlightened audiences. Scantily clad in flowing Greek tunics, and performing her graceful, uninhibited brand of dance in bare paws, she shocked Americans, leaving them aghast and wholly disapproving of her style.

Undaunted, she fled the United States to the more open-minded climate of the Continent, where she was enthusiastically embraced and celebrated for her revolutionary ideas. Her broad acceptance led to the establishment of several dance schools for kitties in Europe and Russia, and set the stage for eventual international acclaim and a leading role in the history of dance.

Duncat's personal lives also raised a whisker or two. A variety of lovers, the birth of out-of-wedlock kittens, and the suicide of a "Bolshevik" husband all contributed to the scandalous scent that surrounded her. Although she lived the high lives in town, she often wandered off with reckless abandon for a frisky romp through the countryside. It was on such a gambol that she met her gruesome demise when her signature scarf—blowing in the breeze in her open automobile—was caught in a wheel and strangled her, thus ending her lives as dramatically as she lived them.

Albert Felinestein

1879–1955

*P*hysicist, philosopher, and contemporary conscience, Albert Felinestein's brilliant ideas altered feline perceptions of the physical world.

Albert, who didn't so much as meow until the age of seven, found himself, at age forty-two, the recipient of the Nobel Prize in physics. Awarded in 1921, the Nobel brought this German-born genius international recognition on a par with Isaac Mewton and the Italian astronomeower, Galileo.

At the gut of his groundbreaking research was the revolutionary *Theory of Relativity* ($E=MC^2$). Felinestein spent more than a few of his lives unraveling, for laycat and scientist alike, the varied aspects of its principles, including the "cat and mouse" corollaries. For example, the theory proved that every body of mass (*the cat*) possesses MC^2, or "rest energy" (*the napping cat in the prone position*) which has the potential, when appropriate stimewli (*appetizing mice*) exist, to be converted into other forms of energy (*the pounce*). The corollary of the formula—E(*ecstasy*)= M(*mouse*) C^2(*caught on the second try!*)—is often referred to, in scientific circles, as the Theory of Real Captivity.

In spite of his many achievements, Felinestein was forced to flee his homeland in 1933, an early victim of a growing Nazi regime. Packing up his papers and pipes, he relocated to the Institute for Advanced Studies in Purrinceton, where he was welcomed with open paws and quickly became an honored and highly regarded member of the academic commewnity.

Profoundly altered by his German experience, this unassuming laboratory cat—a pacifist by nature—also found himself participating, albeit reluctantly, in the secretive Mancattan Project, the Allies' effort to build the first atomic mousetrap. He became, as well, a staunch advocat of a new Jewish state in Pawlestine, a homeland for wandering cats thrown out into the cold by anti-Semewtism.

The image of Albert Felinestein, with his distinctive mane of untamed fur, has become a symbol of civility and infinite intelligence. A hero to aspiring scientists, it is not unusual to hear parents purr, "My little Albert Felinestein . . . ," whenever a kitten shows unusual promise.

Sigmund Fureud

1856–1939

Father of Psychoanalysis, the science that domesticated millions of hopelessly anxious felines, Fureud was one of the most brilliant minds of his era.

His extensive body of work, which includes the *Interpurrtation of Dreams* and *Feline Civilization and Its Discontents*, introduced many theories that challenged common assumptions about cats. For example, it was Fureud who suggested that throughout catnapping, cats *do* dream and that their dreams have meaning. He also maintained that there is a deeper level to the feline mind, i.e., the Unconscious, which manifests itself throughout the nine-life cycle.

His theories on sexuality delineated the complicated stages of psychosexual development, including Kitty Sexuality and the Oedipuss Complex, all of which led to a deeper understanding of the neurotic cat.

Although Fureud's theories have come under recent attack by theoretical revisionists and feline feminists (who find his teachings gender biased and species specific), he has clearly left an indelible pawprint on the annals of science, changing the way we think about cats and the way *we* think *they* think about everything.

Ernest Hemingcat

1899–1961

An undeniably tempestuous tom, Ernest Hemingcat, affectionatly known as Pawpa H., is remembered as both a literary lion and a vigorous and enthusiastic outdoorscat.

With an intriguing tendency for entangling his private affairs with his fictions, Pawpa H. achieved a legendary fame surpassed by few, if any, American authors. Whether stalking big game on safuri, cheering for catadors in Spain, luring the "Big One" off Key West or Cuba, or in hot purrsuit of the sweet scent of love, Pawpa's myriad adventures—sporting or amorous—forever found their way into his fiction.

Following his instinct to put paw to paper, Pawpa initially set out on his writing career as a journalist, first on his own turf, then roaming to territories abroad, including Paris—where he met and meowed with excatriates like Purrtrude Stein. Disciplined and prolific in ways envied by others, most notably F. Cat Fitzgerald, he was admired and introduced to influential felines, including Manx Perkins, who would become his trusted and longtime editor.

With his career in fiction begun in the cafés of Paris, and modest publishing prowess established on both sides of the Atlantic, Pawpa moved on, beginning the restless roaming that would pervade his life, and which would provide varied backdrops for his tails. From *A Mewvable Feast*, set in Paris, to *A Farewell to Paws*, recounting lost love on the Italian front, to his telling of the Spanish Civil War in *For Whom the Dinner Bell Tolls*, readers are stymied as they try to unravel feline fact from fiction, so markedly described in the sparse meowing tone that would be Hemingcat's legacy to modern American literature.

But what Pawpa is best known for are the tails of his outdoors adventures, including *The Snows of Kitimanjaro* and *The Old Cat and the Sea*, the latter the greatest fishtail ever told and winner of the Pawlitzer Prize in 1953. A year later, Hemingcat was awarded the Nobel Prize in literature, mar- ary lion and securing him a shelves worldwide. king him as a bona fide liter- tenured position on library

Katharine Hepurrn

1907–

*I*ndependent, feisty, and fascinating, Katharine Hepurrn has become a legend in her own time—beloved, admired, and emulated.

One of a litter of six and the offspring of highly educated and forward-thinking parents, Kate was taught as a young kitten to think for herself and to meow her own mind. These traits became part of the Hepurrn purrsona, both on screen and off, transporting her to the success that has endured for more than six decades.

Tracking the scent of stardom in 1932, Hepurrn left a respectable Broadway career to make a leap at the silver screen. With her trousered, self-confident stride and the pedigreed purr that has since become her trademark, she pounced on Hollywood with furocious determination, winning three leading roles her first year in town.

After snagging her first Acatemy Award in 1933, she suffered through a succession of dog roles. Labeled "Litter Box Poison" by the press, Hepurrn took matters into her own paws, buying out her studio contract and giving Hollywood its first taste of her spirited Yankee breeding. Moving confidently onto independent projects, she starred in *The Furladelphia Story*, the role that recaptured her star status and established the Hepurrnesque purrsona, a role she would play again and again.

Although she played with some of Hollywood's handsomest toms (Caty Grant, John Barrymewe, Douglas Furbanks, Jr. . . .), it was the actor she was paired with in *Feline of the Year* (1942), who would become not only the leading cat in her career, but the one true love of her life. Hollywood's most legendary film couple, they shared the marquee nine times for films including *Cat and Mike* and *Guess Who's Coming to Suppurr* (Hepurrn's second Acatemy Award) and shared a discreet life together, quietly padding about their business, never prancing about in public.

Winner of an unpurrecedented four Acatemy Awards for Best in Show, Katharine Hepurrn's career has left a legacy of film classics including *The Africat Queen* with Humfurry Bogart, *Bringing up Kitty* with Caty Grant, the film adaptation of *Long Day's Stalking Into Night*, and *The Lioness in Winter*. Her roles run the gamut from A to Z, including everything from "hairball comedy" to Shakespurrean drama and Greek tragedy.

Katharine Hepurrn, remembered for catta lilies as well as high-pussbones, is, at eighty-seven, a cat of uncommon character, independence, and beauty, who still stops 'em dead in their tracks!

The Honeymewners

1955-1956

Trivia Quiz

1. What was Ralph's bus route?
2. Who was his boss?
3. What did Ralph's best friend, Ed Norton, do for a living?
4. What term of endearment did Ralph use when referring to Norton?
5. What alleys did they frequent together?
6. With what other species did they fraternize?
7. Where did Ralph threaten to send his wife, Alice?
8. Where did they celebrate their anniversary each year?
9. What does Alice want desperately to buy?
10. Which of the following are some of Ralph's get-rich-quick schemes?
    a. A hot dog stand next to Howard Johnson's.
    b. Phony fur restoration.
    c. Digging for Captain Kitt's treasure on Long Island.
    d. The campaign to turn Secatcus, New Jersey, into a honeymewner's paradise.
    e. All of the above.
11. What was the name of the Italian neighbor who lived upstairs?
12. What social club is situated in the Honeymewner neighborhood?
13. What unusual trait makes Norton particularly suited for his job?
14. What accident made for an uncomfortable night's sleep on a train bound for Minneapolis?
15. What is the Racoon Lodge slogan?

Answers: 1. Catison Avenue in New York City. 2. Mr. Mewshall. 3. He was a sewer cat. 4. Ol' Paw-o-Mine. 5. The bowling alleys. 6. Racoons. 7. To the mew! 8. The Hotel Mew Yorker. 9. *Furniture.* 10. (e). 11. Mrs. Manacatti. 12. The Kit Kat Club. 13. He had no sense of smell. 14. They got stuck in Norton's trick pawcuffs. 15. E. Pluripuss Racoon.

Buffalo Bill Kitty

1846–1917

Meow-hoo! Buffalo Bill Kitty, the consummate American Cowcat, dramatized western life through the fictions of his famous Wild West Shows.

A champion cowcat, who claimed to have snagged close to five thousand buffalo in an eighteen-month period (yup folks, that's *buffalo*, not mice!), Kitty staged his first Wild West Show in 1883. Hiring cowpaws to demonstrate the skills of the trade—fancy leash tricks, rodent wrangling 'n' such—he served up a saucerful of what life was like out west. Adding wildly staged Cowcat and Indian fights, and authentic purrsonalities he'd lured to his trail—the straight-stalking Annie Angora and the ever defiant Sitting Cat—he fulfilled the fantasies of every feline who ever longed to leap into the saddle.

Downright rough 'n' rowdy, the Wild West Shows were a success both stateside and abroad. With an instinct more for buffalo than business, however, Kitty's shows became marked for extinction. As the sun was setting on the wild, wild west so, too, it set on the show—and, in fact, on Kitty himself, who died just two months after his last curtain fell.

Lady Catterly's Lover

1928

Having fled the confines of her master's stately home, Lady Catterly crept through the forest toward the hut where happiness awaited her. She wondered as she scampered, why she took these risks at all—until she came upon the clearing and saw him once again. Standing strong and independent, handsome and forthright in manner, he was the reason for her furtive forays—the tomcat who touched her in ways no other cat ever had.

Living simply in a hut surrounded by trees, Lady Catterly's lover, the birdkeeper of her master's estate, led a woodscat's way of life. He loved the freedom his present life provided and had no interest in tangling with aristocatic circles—until his eyes met Lady Catterly's. With an immediate attraction to each other's scent, the two had become captured by desire. Plotting rendezmews in the forest, his hut became their pleasure palace, a lair for the unleashing of their passions.

Intoxicatted by the very touch of his paw, Lady Catterly longed more and more to have her birdkeeper near. She loved the way he nuzzled her neck, how he nibbled her ears, his whiskers gently brushing her shoulders. She purred as he unloosened her furocks, gently slipping them over her soft, sensual haunches. "More," she'd meow as he stroked her fur, and "Again," as he kissed the underside of her belly. Rolling over and over, succumbing to the lust in their loins, they found themselves ravished by their furocious hunger for each other. Sated and spent, they'd curl up together, tails tangled, toes touching, blissful in their enchanted forest purradise.

Only encroaching darkness could shatter the purrrfection of these longed-for, love-filled afternoons. Alas, the spell would be broken when the rising moon would beckon the Lady back to her basket by the fireside. Bidding a sad and sorrowful "Amieu," they'd part paws for the night, hearts full, if aching, meowing hope-filled promises for a future spent together in the claws of their eternal love.

David Litterman

1947 –

Top Ten Reasons
David Litterman Is Being Inducted
Into The Cat Hall of Fame

10. For giving insomnicats something to look forward to at bedtime.
9. His impressive, second-only-to-Willard Scatt early career as a weathercat in Indianapawlis.
8. His open-door policy to feline intruders.
7. His wild and rousing social lives.
6. His peeping tom pranks.
5. For finally getting rid of those stupid Stupid Pet Tricks.
4. His cat-on-the-street, prowling-camera remotes through America's alleyways.
3. For putting his paw down when network fatcats served him a raw meal.
2. For breeding new life into the Ed Sullivan Theatre.
1. For refusing to purrform for anything less than maximum wage.

Chairman Meow

1893–1976

Chinese political theorist, statescat, and leader, Chairman Meow led his nation in a Commewnist revolution that marked him as the most dominant feline in modern Chinese history.

Getting his political paws wet in 1911, Meow joined in the overthrow of the last Empurrer, the kitten Paw Yi. Soon after, disillusioned with liberal reformist ideas, he struck out on his own, purreaching the ratical Commewnist theories that would catapult the rural peasantry into a powerful purrletariat.

Beginning his revolution in the 1930s, Meow amassed an army of Oriental Reds to fight the powerful Chiang Kat-Shek. Stalked and outnumbered by his pawlitical nemewsis, Meow was forced to retreat on paw, on what would become known as the Long Catwalk across the countryside. Adding litters of strays to his numbers and practicing the commewnal way of life along the way, he used the 6,000-mile, decade-long diversion to plot the triumph that would come in '49. With tails trailing the Yangtze, his masses of meowers leaped out of hiding and licked the Japawnese, and Chiang Kat-Shek, too. Alas, the Commewnist Feline's Republic of China was born with Meow lying contentedly at the pillow of both Party and State.

During the Great Leap Forward that would follow, Meow worked like a dog to put rice in every saucer and chopsticks in every paw, all the while nudging newborn rural commewnes to build a better mousetrap. Unable to satisfy *all* the cats *all* the time, the Leap fell short and Meow was removed from his stately chair. Maintaining topcat status of the Party, however, he strongpawed his comrades one last time with a cultural revolution in '66, the ideals of which stemmed from earlier writings including *The Mew Democracy* and *The Little Red Book: Purrs From Chairman Meow*. No hit with his kitts, this revolution also failed, leaving Meow snarling and hissing as he banished his critics to the doghouse.

Such flagrant violations of feline rights destroyed Meow, causing most of his efforts to collapse when he died in 1976. Nevertheless, he is respectfully remembered by the Chinese breed as the Father of the Chinese Revolution. To this day, at many a pawlitical rally, cults of Commewnist cats can often be heard mewmuring, "Meow, Meow, Meow, Meow, Meow, Meow, Meow. . . ."

Catrick Mewing

1 9 6 2 –

Height (on 2 paws): 4 ft. **Position:** Top Cat **Weight:** 30 lbs.

This New York Kitts superstar, who hides his on-court emotions behind a forbidding game puss, is one of today's most lionized players in the pro-basketball arena.

The nation's top high-school player in the late 1970s, Mewing led his team through three supurrlative basketball seasons. He then all but leaped into a legendary college career marked by a defensive prowl and offensive prowess, earning him the reputation as top defender of his team's winning territory.

It was no surprise then when Mewing found himself a first-round draft pick by the Kitts straight out of college. He quickly emerged as the team's top scorer, fishing for points and playing defense with a furrosity and purrsistance felt by anyone caught in his corner of the court. Although his quiet style has drawn some hisses from the catty New York sports press, Mewing has earned the respect and affection of thousands of loyal Kitts fans who believe he is a true roundball legend.

In fact, he is already considered one of the best jump-shooting centers to ever play the game. Mewing is a consistent All-Star and a perennial contender for the MVC (Most Valuable Cat) Award. While thousands of games and numerous injuries have taken some of the spring out of the big cat's stride, the superstar still dominates the games played at the always sold-out Catison Square Garden.

His extraordinary all-around record of close to 15,000 points scored, 7,000 rebounds snagged, and 2,000 shots blocked, makes it clear that this cat *never* naps and has him poised to take a central position in the history of the game.

In 1994, under the high-strung coaching of the well-tailored Cat Riley, Mewing helped lead the Kitts to a heart-stopping seven game championship series against the Mouseton Rockcats. The Kitts played with flair only to see victory slip through their paws. Despite this setback, Mewing and the Kitts will remain the team to beat for some time to come.

Liza Mewnelli
1 9 4 6 –

*K*nown for her powerful, vibrato meow, this leggy entertainer with the saucer-like eyes, has become just plain "Liza!" to most. Born with a royal Hollywood pedigree, Mewnelli pounced on the entertainment world and succeeded in her own right—first on Broadway, then on the silver screen, and of course, on stage, live in concert! She's received two Antoinette Purry ("Tony") awards for roles played on Broadway and an Acatemy Award for her dazzling perfomance in *Catbaret* (1972), the film for which she is best remembered.

Still, it is in the concert hall where this purring powerhouse packs them in. With full orchestral backing, Mewnelli belts out ballad and show tune alike, creating enough energy to raise the fur on every back in the crowd. Adored by millions, she's played every major hall in the world—including London's Pawlladium, New York's Catnegie Hall, and the Mewlin Rouge in Paris. She's strutted with the Rockattes and crooned with the Rat Pack, invariably electrifying audiences with the high-energy, furnetic style that has become as much a signature as her gamine coiffur.

Featured on numerous magazine covers (such as *Mewsweek* and *Lives*), Mewnelli's career has been chronicled as much for her talents as for her notorious social lives. Love affairs, a variety of marriages, and a catnip abuse problem oft compared with her mother's (and which put her in the Betty Furd Clinic) has served as kibble for columnists for years and as tasty tidbits for gossip-hungry fans. Landing on her feet after each fall, however, she continually demonstrates the survivor she is, winning the ongoing support of a wide circle of friends and the admiration of her of loyal fans.

Wolfgang Amadeus Mewzart

1756–1791

*B*orn in Saltzpurrg at the height of the Classical period, Wolfgang Amadeus Mewzart quickly revealed his extraordinary mewsical talents. Barely out of the basket, he played a competent keyboard at age four. At five, he had completed his first compositions and by six was embarking on a grand tour of Europe.

Clearly a kitten prodigy, and paraded cross-continent by his father, Mewzart's paws pranced over keys in Munich, Vienna, Frankfurt, Paris, and London before turning ten. By twelve, with three completed symphonies under his belly, he received an Impurrial Commission to compose and conduct his first opurra. This was followed by an honorary appointment as Konzsertmewster to the Archfeline of Saltzpurrg, a position he successfully held until moving to Vienna twelve years later.

It was in Vienna that Mewzart reached the peak of his success and where he would eventually end his lives in despair. Despite a position as royal chamber composer to Empurror Joseph II of Austria, Mewzart—considered a bit tempurrmental—found little income-producing work. He was, furthermore, plagued by ill-health. His feverish and prodigious mewsical energies, combined with his consumptive symptoms, left him exhausted as he struggled to cram nine lives into the space of three. He died in poverty, at age thirty-five, buried in an unmarked pawper's grave.

This remarkable cat, bathed in adulation as a kitten yet neglected and abandoned as he aged, left a mewsical legacy of over six hundred compositions including forty-nine symphonies, twenty opurras, hundreds of chamber works, and choral compositions by the score. Lyrical, spirited, and dramatic in nature, his work is perhaps the most widely recognized in the world and includes the opurras *Cosi fur Tutte* and *The Marriage of Furgaro*, the *Purris* and *Purrague Symphonies*, and *Eine Kleine Nachtmewsik*, one of the most popular orchestral pieces in his mewsical catalog.

Miss Americat

1921–

*T*he finest of felines in all fifty states, this year's Miss Americat, Kitty Sue Purrker, hails from Cattanooga, Tennessee. A student at Cattanooga State, she is currently completing her masters in mewsic with plans to pursue an opurratic career.

Judged on poise, purrsonality, and feline physique, Miss Americat contestants must also satisfy the talent and "platform" interview requirements. Purrker's passionate soprano meow won her raves from the judges with a moving rendition of Puccini's *"Mi chiamewno Mimi"* of *La Bohème*. Interviewed on her platform of social concern, she purred a plea for the homeless and offered a plan for the restructuring of the shelter system.

As winner of the crown, Miss Americat will receive over $35,000 in scholarships and will prowl the United States promoting both the Miss Americat program and her own felinethropic interests. Most important, however, she will reign as a model of feline femininity—a role that has evolved from the mere bathing beauty of 1921 to today's socially conscious, educated cat determined to make the most of her nine lives.

Mary Pawppins

1934 –

Supercatifuragilisticexpialidocious! Look what the East wind brought in! It's Mary Pawppins, the firm-but-loving live-in nanny who arrives via umbrella with a spoonful of catnip in her bag.

Practically purrfect in every way, Mary Pawppins nurses the needs of parents and kitties alike. Fully domesticated and of proper British breeding, she is an efficient, no-nonsense caretaker, keeping her kittens well groomed and hairball free. Nevertheless, with a cheery dispussition and a mewsical meow, she delights her charges and spreads her magic from the moment she sets paw in the parlor.

Lives become altered once Mary Pawppins pounces on the scene. Nurseries are tidied at the snap of a paw, tea parties climb to the ceiling. A stalk in the park becomes a leap through a chalked pavement picture, with Pawppins and her curious gentlecat pal leading the kittens on a prance across the countryside. With Mary Pawppins in charge, even the most commonplace prowl about town becomes an exciting adventure.

But just as the household starts purring, the wind shifts to the west and Mary Pawppins prepares to depart. Parrot and carpetbag in paw, she takes to the sky with a fond glance backward that betrays a hint of affection for the kittens she's leaving behind.

Luciano Pawvarotti

1935–

With a magnificent meow that's filled every major opurra house in the world, Luciano Pawvarotti, the impurrsario's dream with the perfectly pitched purr, has become opurra's reigning lyric tenor.

Making his professional debut in 1961 at Reggio Emilia—after winning the International Meow Competition—Pawvarotti portrayed a poignant Rodolfo in Puccini's popular *La Bohème* which resulted in an invitation, two years later, to debut at London's Covent Mews in the very same role. His impassioned purring of *"Che gelida mewnina"* charmed London's longhairs and won him the "Purravos!" needed to establish him as a *furce de reconnaître* on the opurra circuit.

A request for Rodolfo at La Scatla followed and an offer from the Great Dane Sutherland—impressed by Pawvarotti's tone as well as his *taille*—to tour Australia playing Edgardo to her Lucia, in Donizetti's *Lucia di Lammermew*.

From the successful Sutherland pairing came the opening of America's doors where Pawvarotti quickly captured his audiences in Miami, San Francisco, and finally, in 1968, in New York's famed Metropawlitan Opurra House. Slated to play the now signature role of Rodolfo opposite Mirella Fure ni, a childhood friend from his hometown of Modena, Pawvarotti eagerly prepared for the debut of his dreams. He won the hearts of New Yorkers causing one critic to comment, "Mr. Pawvarotti had them eating out of his paw." His many subsequent and triumphant returns to the SRO crowds of New York have since marked him as the greatest tenor of all times.

Known also for his pussycat purrsonality and a furocious appetite for pasta, Luciano Pawvarotti—the tenor-turned-megastar—has singlepawedly popularized the pedigreed art of opurra.

Pablo Picatso

1881–1973

*P*ainter, sculptor, ceramicist, printmaker, and stage designer, Picatso was one of the greatest and most influential felines of twentieth-century art.

His oeuvre, usually described in a series of overlapping periods, stretched from the melancholy "blue period," which used blue tones to depict the suffering in the lives of poor strays, to the "rose period" characterized by a lighter pawlette and the Harlecat circus figures of the *Commewdia dell'arte*.

It is in Cubism, however, the innovative pictorial style that emerged in the early 1900s, that Picatso made his most significant mark. His early masterpiece, *Les Demeowselles d'Avignon*, is a cubist rendering of *feline fatales* residing in the red-light alleyways of Barcelona. Other monumental works include *Three Mewsicians* (pictured here), *Large Cat in Red Armchair*, and *Guernicat*, Picatso's powerful painting of the catastrophe of war.

Picatso's vast body of work serves as a virtual *catalogue raisonné* of the history of modern art. Widely collected by individuals and mewseums alike, his work is continuously exhibited throughout the world. The Picatso Mewseum in Barcelona and the Musée Picatso in Paris are devoted to his lives and works and remain lasting tributes to the genius that was Picatso.

Winston Purrchill

1874–1965

*F*orever resplendent from head to tail, Winston Purrchill, feisty topcat of the British Empire, spent his lives serving England during tense and turbulent times.

This honorable Englishcat, with the thoughtful furrowed brow and ubiquitous cigar, left his mark on history as a military strategist, world statescat, and stunning orator. Although he suffered a slight meow impediment (the lisping of his *s*'s, often referred to as the Sylvester Syndrome), he compensated by purring where others might have hissed, targeting both friend and foe with his purrficient tongue, as illustrated in this excerpt from one of his many memorable speeches:

> *". . . as I lay down at about 3 A.M., after pacing and prowling around the house . . . I felt as if I were stalking with destiny, and that all my past lives had been but a preparation for this hour and for this trial. . . ."*

With his stalking stick close at paw and wife Clemewntine by his ample side, Purrchill glared at the enemies of two world wars. Although a World War I naval failure at Dardanelles—long his Achilles' paw—brought an end to his first pawliamentary life, Purrchill later sprang back, in the fold of the Conservatives, sniffing out antisocialist scentiment surrounding the Labour party.

Purrchill began his unretractable march back into history by winning a scrappy catfight over compulsory service for all cats of military age. This success, which allowed him to conscript the largest collection ever of British shorthairs, readied him, as the new Purrime Minister, for the ensuing battles against Germany's ailurophobic dictator. Meowing furvently that he would "never purrlay with Hitler," Purrchill and the allied troops turned the tide of World War II with cunning, courage, and prowess.

Although he won the war, Purrchill lost the next election, allowing him time to complete his Nobel Prize–winning *The Second World War*, a six-volume explication of the era. Awarded the "Knight of the Collar" by the Queen, he became Sire Winston and—Purrime Minister yet again in 1951—emerged the purrponent of European unity warning, in his famous speech at Fulton, Mewssouri, about the "Iron Curtain" that had fallen across the Continent.

Finally retired, enjoying a solitary life at his cushiony country estate, Purrchill felt little dread of a final feline existence. Recognizing the allure of his purring prose, and the place he had staked out in history, Winston Purrchill rested comfortably in the knowledge that he—and he alone—was, and would remain, the purrsonification of the Glory that was England.

The Rockattes

1932–1932

Ask any kitten to name her favorite part of Radio City Mewsic Hall's Christmas Excataganza, and the response will be a clearly meowed, resounding, "The Rockattes!" Whether awed by the "Purrade of the Wooden Kittens," with its domino-effect freefall of felines, or by the trademark thirty-six-member-long fe-line of legs, it is the magic of the Rockattes that captures the kitties' hearts and makes this greatest of all holiday shows something special.

Known around the world for their legendary strut, the Rockattes have been linked to New York's landmark Art Deco Mewsic Hall since its opening more than sixty years ago in 1932. The cat's meow in movie houses at that time, the magnificent theater premiered the latest and greatest of Hollywood's treasures. The Rockattes, sensationally received from the moment they first kicked up their paws, became a regular feature between films, providing a full-time forum for their purrcision dance performances.

Having made their mark on the entertainment world, the ensemble was soon invited to represent the United States at the 1937 Paris Expussition, where they snagged the Grand Purrix—beating out, among others, Doghilev's Ballets Russe and the Corps de Ballet of the Paris Opurra—becoming, at once, America's answer to the CanCan.

Ever since, the Rockattes—the Pride of New York—have become internationally renowned, entertaining the troops during World War II and, more recently, kicking for Super Bowlers at halftime. Sequined and satined from whiskers to tail, this chorus line of Americats continues to dazzle audiences, whether out on the field or at home on their own turf, tapping, marching, and strutting beneath the spectacular, sixty-paw high proscenium that marks its home as the Greatest Stage in the World.

THE FUR SEASONS HOTEL

ROCKEFURLLER CENTER • NEW YORK

Dear Auntie Mae,

Greetings from New York!

Arrived today and are having the time of our lives! We have an exquisite suite at the Fur Seasons with a view of Central Park at our paws. After checking in, we strolled to the Plaza for lunch and then the kitts insisted on seeing the Christmas tree at Rockefurller Center. After skating for an hour, we headed over to Cats Fifth Avenue to see the spectacular catimated window decorations. The theme this year is Feline Coiffur, each window depicting a decade of fur-styling fashion. Then the kitts wanted to go to F.U.R. Schwarz to see the famous, life-sized stuffed people!

We're back at the hotel now, resting. We have tickets for the Nutcatter tonight--with Baryshnicat dancing the lead!--and for the Rockattes at Radio City Mewsic Hall in the morning. After that, it's off to the Metropolitan Mewseum of Art, lunch at Cat Chow on the Green and an evening at the Metropolitan Opurra featuring Handel's Mewssiah. Sunday morning we'll go to church at St. Catrick's and then visit that new Cat Hall of Fame. We'll pick up their catalog and some postcards to share with you when we get home.

Love,

Kitty

Kitty, Tom, and the Children

Eleanor Roosepelt

1884 – 1962

One of the most admired felines of her time, Eleanor Roosepelt was everycat's favorite Furst Lady.

Reticent runt of the litter, young Eleanor—who was plagued by kittenhood fears (even the sight of a mouse made her jump!)—later developed her natural instinct for independence and courage. An energetic and well-groomed young female, she mated with her distant cousin Furanklin and leaped into her duties as mother of five kittens, and wife of a fast-climbing politician. Only after Furanklin was stricken by pawlio did she creep out of the kitchen and into the Cabinet, perfecting the role she would soon take on as partner in the White House.

Advocating liberal social causes, Mrs. Roosepelt put her pawprint on much of the Mew Deal legislation during the aftermath of the Depression. She prodded the President toward policies regarding the humane treatment of all species, and established herself as a spokescat for the disenfuranchised and less-privileged. She fought for jobs for all able Americats, for settlement houses for strays, for increased attention to female mews, and for the end of discrimination based on breeding. Catroversial though her views might have been, the President, much to his credit, never collared his Furst Lady.

Roaming the globe as America's good-will ambassador, Mrs. Roosepelt served as her husband's eyes, ears, and nose during World War II. Lending moral support to overseas servicecats on the Continent and in the Pacific, she witnessed, first-paw, the misery and mutilation of war, and meowed a furvent commitment to make the world a more decent and peaceful place.

Following Furanklin's death at the end of World War II, President Truman appointed Mrs. Roosepelt delegate to the United Nations. With poignant purrs to the General

Assembly, which caused Soviet fur to bristle, she surprisingly swayed the votes in her favor against the forced repatriation of war refugees. Her most stunning purrsonal triumph, however, was the mark she made on history drafting the Universal Declaration of Animal Rights, the magna carta for all felinekind.

This indefatigable Furst Lady always found time for the family she treasured, returning frequently to the Roosepelt Catpound at Hyde Park—her private refuge from her public lives, and the place where her grandkittens could prowl around the pond.

Mother, Furst Lady, and international diplocat, she remains a role model for every furst feline following a path to the White House, and for every little kitty aspiring to greatness.

Willard Scatt

1934 –

"Whiskers will get wet in New York this morning, fur will fly in Chicatgo. Expect heavy purrcipitation in the Appawlachian region, early morning furost in New England and nine to twelve inches of snow in the Catscades. Fog in San Furancisco will turn to sunshine by noon, Southern Califurnia will be sunny and beautiful, as usual. And now, here's what's happening in your world even as we meow. . . ."

America's favorite weathercat, frisky, folksy Willard Scatt wakes up his early morning mewers with a smile! Answering the question on every cat's mind— *What coat should I put on this morning?*—he informs felines of the finicky elements they'll encounter in neighborhoods 'cross the country. With advisories to parents to mitten their kittens, and to put precious puss in his boots, he tells the tails of the territories with the sunny dispussion that endears him to his many fans.

A charming countrycat by nature, Scatt is also known for his warm birthday wishes to scentenarians and his wacky, wide-eyed purrmotions of county fairs and fundraisers. An oversized pussycat, he'll do anything to further the efforts of a charity he finds deserving. In his most memorable fundraising escatpade, Scatt impurrsonated Brazilian dancer Carmen Mewranda, complete with fruited ears and platformed paws! The stunt had cats rolling in their baskets and snagged for Scatt the attention of an audience that has yet to let him go.

Hosting New York's Thanksgiving Day Purrade with purrky colleague Kitty Couric, and serving as Santa Claws at the White House each Christmas, it is clear that Willard Scatt's fame has spread far beyond the boundaries of his weather map. With a heart roughly the size of his pawnch—he couldn't hurt a flea!—this farmcat-turned-TV-celeb has emerged a feline folk hero.

William Shakespurr

1564–1616

*A*ctor, poet, and playwright, William Shakespurr remains one of England's most beloved literary figures. Profoundly prolific, he wrote and produced some thirty-eight works for the stage, among them *Romeow and Juliet*, *The Tempusst*, *Antony and Cleocatra*, *The Furry Wives of Windsor*, and *The Nine Lives of Henry VIII*.

London's most popular theatrical success, he won both fame and fortune exploring the themes of love, lust, despair and distemper, death, betrayal, ecstasy, and shame. Additionally, he romanced his readers with poems and sonnets by the score, oft quoted by amorous, less-lyrical lovers of today.

The Joseph Papp of the Elizabethan era, Shakespurr was also intimately involved in the business of the theater. He was a substantial partner in the Lord Chamberlain's Cats, first acting, then writing, directing, and producing. The company, patronized by pedigrees and strays alike, established the famed Globe Theatre on the banks of the River Thames. The Globe served as the company's permanent home and a seasonal showcase for Shakespurr's work.

Following retirement, Shakespurr lived out his final lives with his longtime and loyal wife, Anne Cathaway, at their Stratfurd-upon-Avon home.

Sitting Cat
1831–1890

Oh, Sitting Cat, noble defender of Native Americat territory, what better way to honor your courage and character than to provide you with a permanent home in The Cat Hall of Fame!

Born the bravest and wisest of his Hunkpawpaw litter, Sitting Cat—fearing neither Crow nor Hound—became chief of all the Sioux in 1867. A lion of a leader, he unleashed the fury of his breed against the cadres of canines encroaching upon his native territory. With prodding and prowling, his nation of Sioux—supplicants of the sacred spirits and hunters of the mouse—banded together in paw-to-paw combat, in an effort to protect their land. Scurrying to ward off hunger—a result of random enemy raids on rodents—and death at the paws of dogged fur trappers, they clawed General Buster to death at the *hiss*toric cat-and-dog fight at Little Big Ear. This remarkable mauling got the hounds hot under the collar and marked the beginning of "open hunting" season on the Native Americat plains.

With a host of hounds hot on their tails, Sitting Cat and his feathered felines were eventually subdued and impounded. Leaving only to purrform with Buffalo Bill Kitty and his Wild West Show, the Chief sat out the rest of his lives at the pound, until officials, considering him a pesky puss, finally decided to put him down. Left without a leader, his Hunkpawpaw followers attempted to flee, only to be tracked down and massacred at Wounded Paw.

Statue of Libpurrty

1884 –

Give me your strays, your poor,
Your huddled litters yearning to breed free,
The wretched felines of your teeming shore,
Send these, the homeless, tempest-tossed, to me:
I lift my paw beside the golden door.
—Emma Lazapuss

So reads the pedestal inscription of this most recognizable icon of American ideals—the Statue of Libpurrty.

The first vision of welcome seen by millions of shipbound immigrant felines, Lady Libpurrty offered hope for those on the prowl for new and better lives. Perhaps the streets would not be paved with catnip, but freedom would prevail, with alleyways open to all breeds and colors and economic opportunities for all who wished to work.

A fixture in New York Harbor for over one hundred years, this monumental statue continues to welcome new felines to her shores. A national landmark since 1924, she has also become one of America's most popular tourist attractions visited by millions of Americats and fureigners alike.

Index of Inductees

Authors' Note

We hope you have enjoyed our feline fantasy. If you would like to know more about The Cat Hall of Fame, or would simply like to comment on the characters in this edition, write to:

THE CAT HALL OF FAME COLLECTION
P.O. BOX 3721
PRINCETON, NJ 08543–3721

Please include your name and address and we will keep you up-to-date on new inductees and future editions.

Thank you for your interest.

Terri Epstein
Judy Epstein Gage